# LYFT

by

# ANONYMOUS

# Copyright

First Edition, 2016, manufactured in USA
1 2 3 4 5 6 7 8 9 10 LSI 20 19 18 17 16
Set in Times New Roman

International Standard Book Number:
ISBN 978-0-9913381-4-6

Wake Up Inc
PO Box 4251,
Westminster, CA, 92684

www.bestsellerguru.com
www.thedriverstories.com

# CONTENTS

## Who Wrote This Book?

This book represents all the Drivers worldwide, all colors and all languages—the moms and dads that are driving for a second job to support their families, the college students that are driving to pay their tuition. The drivers that are in between jobs and for those that are driving for cash flow to support their own dream.

Enjoy the book.

# ABOUT JOHNNY

Johnny moved to Hollywood. He was a natural, so it made a lot of sense. He would become the next champion of the silver screen, like a Leonardo DiCaprio, Christian Bale, Tom Cruise, Brad Pitt, George Clooney, or maybe even a Sharito Copley.

The reason it made so much sense was that Johnny was such a great athlete in school.

Everybody said that he was a pro quarterback and top rung if there ever was one. But he just didn't get it. Go out to the smelly gym. Meet up with a bunch of smelly dudes. Put on a smelly outfit.

He did enjoy busting heads when they snuck past the linemen and tried to grab him. But even stiff arming, kicking, and knocking down boring guys gets old fast. Where was the glitz, the warmth, and the girls? He decided that sports were just not his calling in life.

Johnny never really wanted to pursue a life as a professional athlete even though the coach was always after him to do so. One day, he and Smitty, the coach, were walking in the hall when they approached Ed Hastings, the high school drama teacher. Coach Smitty stuck out his hand and Johnny stuck out his.

And that was that; he was discovered right there. When he heard the word drama, a word that is simple and ordinary, while paused from walking in the halls, he felt all warm and fuzzy. He could imagine all of those beautiful girls he saw at the movies.

The drama coach invited him to stop by the auditorium. As he got closer, he could hear a beautiful girl giving a very intense speech. She seemed so real that Johnny forgot she was just "acting." The character's name was Abigail, and she was talking to some other girls on the stage. He forgot to focus on how pretty they were. Johnny didn't quite know what was happening yet, but he was mesmerized by her words:

> "...And mark this. Let either of you breathe a word, or the edge of a word, about the other things, and I will come to you in the black of some terrible night and I will bring a pointy reckoning that will shudder you. And you know I can do it; I saw Indians smash my dear parents' heads on the pillow next to mine and I have seen some reddish work done at night, and I can make you wish you had never seen the sun go down!"

It was almost as if Johnny was watching some crazy version of the movie *Mean Girls*, but instead, this was really serious. The student actors then set up for another scene, this time with a boy in the lead of "John Proctor" reciting a passage from some play that gave Johnny the chills. It was more intense than watching the pretty girls:

> "Because it is my name! Because I cannot have another in my life. Because I am not worth the dust on the feet of them that hang! How may I live without my name? I have given you my soul, leave me my name!"

Johnny began to understand what was happening here, even before the drama instructor explained what was going on. The girl, Abigail, was dishonest and manipulating her friends—blackmailing them. The man, John Proctor, was asking forgiveness, obviously speaking, pleading for his life in front of a court of some kind.

He told this to the drama instructor, who said, "That's right on, Johnny, you have good acting instincts. The name of this play is *The Crucible*, by the famous playwright Arthur Miller. It caused quite a stink when it was first performed and to this day—more than 50 years after it was first performed, it still stirs people up, for lots of different reasons. This is the sign of a good play, and the fact that the actors made you *feel something* means they are doing their job."

Johnny left the auditorium, head swirling and full of awe. He went to the library and immediately checked out the play and read it cover to cover several times. He read the background on it, and how Arthur Miller had written it as an allegory; The Salem Witch Trials were just like the McCarthy Hearings in the 1950's and vice versa. Not only was Johnny learning about plays and acting, but he was also learning new history, and it didn't suck like some of his classes did! Acting

was what he wanted to do; this was the job that, if *done well*, would teach people and impact them, and make them feel.

The thing about Johnny was that he was a charismatic, 6-foot-2, blue-eyed, All-American white boy type, with dark brown hair. Everyone said he looked like Brad Pitt when he was in *Thelma and Louise*. He was fit with a chiseled body and one of those pretty-boy, sunshine smiles that could light up a whole room. In addition to his physical good looks, Johnny also had a very kind and loving personality. He was such a warm guy that most people fell deeply in love with him and his personality, even the smelly dudes in the locker room.

Johnny was raised by a single mom, who he credits with giving him a kind and loving personality. She actually glowed with kindness, and she always encouraged him to do what he loved to do. Mom also taught Johnny how to protect himself. She carefully explained to him that in the end, time was all he had. She told him that his time was more valuable than she could say. Johnny, though only six, understood what she said immediately.

Since that first teaching session with Mom, Johnny always felt that working for money was

trading his time for what the boss needed, not what Johnny wanted to get done. And that whole trade off always felt like a prison, like the Matrix had snared Johnny.

After his first job working for a nasty-talking old redneck at a nursery, he dumped a load of steer manure on the guy's shiny cowboy boots, and threw down the wheelbarrow. As he walked out into the beautiful Oregon morning, Johnny made a promise to himself that he would only do jobs that he loved and enjoyed.

He grew up in a small town in Oregon, so Johnny was truly a nature boy who loved hiking, skiing, fishing, sitting under a shade tree reading a book, or just lying back gazing at the sky. But when he found out about the world of drama, not long after the Coach Smitty introduced him to the drama teacher, he knew that he must pursue his calling to become a famous actor.

He also felt his destiny was much bigger than his small Oregon town called Bend. No, he had something bigger that he must follow, a bigger dream than his hometown could provide; a destiny with much bigger drama. He knew that Hollywood was his path.

Johnny's first minutes in Hollywood were so exciting he couldn't have expressed it. He was living the dream for sure. He was right in the center of the drama. This was where it all happened and his destiny was right around each corner.

Of course, Hollywood was much different than his little town in Oregon. It was the big, noisy, out-of-control, concrete and asphalt, harsh and grating, materialistic city. At home, the pace was slower and things were simpler, but here in the heart of the entertainment industry everything seemed so insensitive. Unlike back home, people in Hollywood were all trying to cover up their insecurities by creating fake personalities for themselves.

One quality Johnny had always been capable of in a flash was reading people and knowing instantly what they desired. People told him that he was psychic and very intuitive. Even as a young child, he could always sense if a person was good or held on to bad energy.

His mom taught him to always find one good thing in each person and even if a person was bad, to go the extra mile, reach deep down inside himself, and find that special good thing inside the bad egg.

Johnny's mother had said that deep down inside all humans were always good, but because the environment around them had been harsh and hard times had come and gone, they had put walls up to protect themselves. His mom was a very beautiful lady with a huge smile and a beautiful singing voice. She used to sing the old Earth Wind & Fire song for him:

"That's the Way of the World"
By Charles Stepney, Maurice White, Verdine White

You will find peace of mind
If you look way down in your heart and soul
Don't hesitate 'cause the world seems cold
Stay young at heart 'cause you're never (never, never, ..) old at heart

That's the way of the world
Plant your flower and you grow a pearl
A child is born with a heart of gold
The way of the world makes his heart grow cold

Hearts of fire creates love desire
Take you high and higher to the world you belong

Hearts of fire
Love desire
Higher and higher

Johnny's mom said, "God lives in everyone, but we have to choose to let God shine through us."

Johnny really liked knowing that he could have God shine through him and also guide and lead him to good people. He respected all religions and did not judge anybody's belief, but knew that God was with him, guiding him to stay on a purposeful path.

Johnny was so good at reading people that he didn't even have to try to do it. He just knew people's desires and feelings and could really feel their true energy clearly and precisely. It was just like when he was quarterbacking a football play and knew what all the smelly guys were doing.

He always remembered a quote from a book by a famous writer that said, "You speak so loudly when you walk into the room that you don't even need to say a word."

He could never remember the writer's name, but the thought always stuck in his mind. He could see a guy walking into a big room, where he commanded attention and applied this vision to himself, now that he had arrived in Hollywood.

Because Johnny had always been able to SEE people completely, he realized that all people put out energy. Some people broadcast from a low energy field because of fear, anger, frustration, not being able to trust, or being skeptical. The majority of humans were stuck in those negatives, draining their energy.

But there were a few who remained in high energy flow because they stayed with what they actually wanted, rather than being stuck like the low energy people, who kept thinking about what they didn't want. For example, Johnny could see right through the many women who were always thinking about how they don't want to meet another jerk for a boyfriend, or the vast majority of people who continually thought that they didn't have enough money. Intuitively, Johnny knew that what we focus on would continue to expand and eventually come into our real world.

At an early age, Johnny learned to sit quietly, meditate, and be one with God. He had trained his mind to be silent so it could be happy for no reason at all. And then he trained it to focus on the things he appreciated in the now, right there in each moment, like his health, whatever money he had in his pocket, his freedom and the love he had for his family and friends.

As a boy, along with his mom's wonderful teachings, he had an uncle who gave him the same kind of wisdom about the way of the world.

He and his uncle had watched and savored an old movie many times, *Zorba the Greek*. His uncle would say, "That is how to live your life Johnny; live it like Zorba. Learn to be happy both in the low times and the high times, it is all the same."

Johnny was always good with his money— even as a young kid—at living within his means, while using the money he had to make his life situations work despite being frugal. He even had fun. Johnny learned the art of saving as well. This was how he was able to move to Hollywood to pursue his acting career.

Johnny was aware that this transition would cost him a lot of money to live fully, which was a requirement. He knew that he had to hang out at all of the just-right, hip places in Hollywood, sign up for all of the right acting classes, and that in the beginning, he would be doing a lot of free work, as well as paying for the acting lessons.

Johnny understood inside that his savings would not cover all these expenses, so he needed the right job to keep a cash flow coming into his life. The only way to keep his savings habit flourishing was to always keep cash coming in. He had always known that the only time life became a huge struggle was when you desperately need other people to help you.

This desperation can cause serious mistakes, which could set a person back in the pursuit of their goals. When you have enough cash flow, you always have a choice to walk away from any situation. Johnny had often watched how people treated homeless people on the street. They might give them some change or a buck or two, but most people deep down looked down on them because of their own insecurities. Johnny knew that he would never beg for anything in life and always had the right to walk away because he was his own man and owned his freedom.

With his need for a job to bolster his savings, Johnny started hearing about the new ride sharing services like Lyft and a few other ones. He also heard that these companies were hiring.

Johnny met a guy at an ultra-hip vegetarian restaurant in the LA area called Au Lac, and the guy said he was making OK money driving for a ride-sharing company each day. Johnny already had the perfect fuel economy vehicle; a Toyota hybrid, Prius, that met all the desired qualities and correct specifications to be eligible for one of the ride services.

The concept was an ideal fit with his need for a lot of free time for his acting. He saw clearly that he could be his own boss and work the hours that he wanted to work. It was the perfect cash flow, and it was also a fit with Johnny's desire to see more of California. Right on the spot, he decided, yes, he would become a DRIVER.

# CHAPTER 1

## JOHNNY'S FIRST RIDE IN HOLLYWOOD

Johnny got his clearance to drive and start earning money to beef up his savings, which was drying up a lot faster in Hollywood than it ever had in Oregon. He tapped the Drivers App, and in 2 minutes flat it started beeping, urging him to pick up his first ride. He looked at the app, and the map and routing directed him toward the local high school. He revved up his ride, checked his appearance in the mirror, and started following the directions from the GPS.

Things heated up immediately. He didn't have a clue how he was going to recognize his customer. Who the heck was he supposed to pick up? Out in the front of the school, at the asphalt turn in for waiting, there were about a million angry looking moms and dads hovering over their steering wheels. The whole place swarmed with hormone-charged, totally revved up spoiled brats as wild as small bucking broncos high on methamphetamine.

The app said Johnny was 900 feet away from his target. Then he was wedged into the line, surrounded by of all these cars swarming with high-wired pubescent catastrophes bouncing around like short-circuited bobble heads and their enraged parental units along with a few other, scattered cabbies.

On the app his destination now read 600 feet, but his quiet little Toyota Prius stood at a dead stop. He wished he was in a Porsche or a big muscle car that made a hell of a lot of noise. Bloodthirsty parents surrounded his petite, torpid ride—oh to be in a military Humvee with a blade on the front for pushing things—in their cars, starting to stand down on their horns like threatened hornets. Then the parents began to attack one another. They got down on their horns with overwhelming noise, a cacophony of sound that made Johnny long for a country road in Oregon.

The lady in the car in front of him began flipping off the car in front of her and they started yelling at each other. In the same instant, Johnny noticed a group of 3 young girls walking towards his car, and he thought that they might be his first customers, but they kept walking.

He could hear the girls giggling as they said, "That guy is so cute! I love him."

The cars in front of Johnny started to move when he noticed on the app that the rider's name was Skylar. The app was new so he thought he would learn more about it as he got more experience.

He was not sure if the name Skylar was a girl

or a boy's, but right then a tall, slender, handsome boy looking very smart walked toward his car and asked if he was the driver called Johnny. Johnny assumed that the app told the new passenger everything, including the color and type of car, and the driver's name.

Skylar hopped in the back seat and Johnny entered his return destination and the app said seven miles away. He looked in the back seat and his 1st rider had headphones on and was already texting away on his phone. Johnny thought of making conversation, but his intuition told him to let it be and drive.

He proceeded to the destination, and as fast as he arrived, Skylar jumped out and said, "Thanks a lot dude."

Skylar looked Johnny right in the eye, smiled, and gave him a $10 tip.

Johnny started laughing and looked right at Skylar, who winked at him and said, "Have you ever had the realization that life is never about the destination; it is always about the journey?"

The young guy spun on his feet and shot into the house before Johnny could do anything. Johnny swiped the app, which read $4.27 for the trip and with a $10 dollar tip. Not bad for his first ride.

As Johnny cruised slowly down the street, looking at the picture of Alexander Hamilton on the $10 bill, he knew he was into the right thing, and that he was fully on his path.

# CHAPTER 2

## ROSE AND THE HOUSE OF CARDS

The next few weeks were wild for Johnny. He bounced around Hollywood from one Airbnb to another. It was a very busy time. Not only was he searching for the right place to live, but at the same time, he was signing up for the right acting classes.

He was also interviewing agents, moving from one to another and trusting his intuition. This may be perceived as a little trick most people think is reserved for the fairer sex, but Johnny's mom had taught him how to use it really well. The first agent was a short guy built like a bowling ball. He was mostly bald and had tried to fit himself into a very stylish Italian suit, which didn't work at all.

The agent kept saying: "Uh Huh, I see. Uh Huh, I see," over and over and over, again and again and again.

Finally Johnny stuck out his hand and shook the agent's hand. Johnny could feel that this guy was not what he was looking for. He felt his insincerity and lack of purpose. Johnny turned and walked out the door.

One of the few things Johnny's uncle had taught him was that you don't hang around listening to people who have nothing good to say about you.

He recalled that his uncle had taken him out on one of his birthdays to "let the Turkey fly."

This meant to get really shit-faced drunk on Wild Turkey premium whiskey.

After the old man was good and plotzed, he explained to Johnny in a good bit of detail that all women could be manipulative, and the better looking they are—like Johnny's mom—the more they use the magnetic power of feminine good looks to make the guy do whatever they want.

Johnny had been well trained by his mom to take his uncle's advice with a grain of salt.

His uncle used to say, "You just don't listen to anybody but a little bit. Most people are completely full of shit. They are real lonely and they just talk to hear their own voice so they feel like they have some company. So you gotta be able to leave in a flash."

But Johnny understood deep spiritual thoughts automatically. He never really had to think about the subject. He just knew how to be spiritual and how to accept the good parts of all people, and set the rest aside. Johnny knew how to walk right out the door on the round man in the chichi Italian suit.

The days whirred by like crazy, and with his natural sense for money inherited from his mom, Johnny knew that he needed to settle in so he could hold on to his funds. While he was taking the agent meetings and going to drama events, Johnny began to look for a business coach.

Johnny drove about 5 hours a day and picked up all types of people. The fares were his bread and butter for the most part, and kept him out of his savings. He wouldn't get rich being a DRIVER, but he realized that not only would it protect his savings, it would somehow lead to adventure and success. After a couple of direct deposits, DRIVER paychecks were put into his checking account and a bit into savings, he felt more grounded.

And the job WAS really cool. It kinda felt like Johnny was simply driving around the Los Angeles Basin picking up friends, then driving them around for a while, getting bored with their chatter and dropping them off.

He enjoyed the whole thing. It was fun, and he met this really cool lady that became one of his regular riders. What he liked best was that she had really good energy. They chatted a lot, and she told Johnny about a mansion that her aunt owned in Brentwood, a wealthy part of town. She gave Johnny her aunt's phone number to see if he could possibly live there and help her out.

This was really great news because Johnny wanted to live in one of the big, beautiful homes he passed every day while doing his job. He could easily imagine how good it would feel to go home to the sense of abundance in his life, and that feeling of prosperity would be very important for his acting career.

When he first came to Hollywood, Johnny searched Airbnb, the site and app where you reserve a room that is like staying in a hotel but only your room is right inside people's homes. He found a cheap room on Airbnb, but even though it was cheaper than a hotel, it was way too much per month. He couldn't have savings and a room that he had to keep paying out so much for. It drove him nuts every day, because his mom had made him so good with money. It was instinctive, like a dog going after his bone. Johnny knew that he needed to make smart moves with his cash flow. People up in Oregon weren't kidding—it cost a lot to live in LA.

After Johnny dropped off the cool lady, he called her aunt immediately. She picked the phone right up, and he introduced himself, telling her about knowing her niece, and she said that if her niece gave Johnny her phone number, he must be a good, loving, and caring man.

She asked if he could stop by in an hour and he said, "yes."

Being a deeply spiritual guy, he got off the phone and felt very happy knowing he was on the right path, and God was guiding him.

When he got to her house he was amazed.

All he could say was, "Wow!!!"

Quickly followed by, "What a beauty."

Then, the instant he knocked at the big, carved door it opened slowly. Her name was Rose and she looked to be around 75 or even 80 years old.

Johnny could tell that she had a good heart, and that she was very kind. He felt a warm attraction to her instantly, and it was obvious that the feelings were mutual. A healthy young Asian man in some sort of a cobalt blue silk martial arts uniform served tea with a delicate porcelain service. They sipped a bit and then Rose showed him the house and took him through the magical gardens spilling out from behind the big, elegant home.

As their conversation moved along, Johnny explained that he'd met her niece DRIVING, and had told him that she needed someone to DRIVE her places occasionally. They were soon off on another tangent of their effortless conversation. Talking about nutrition and health came naturally to both of them and it was obvious that the subject carried great mutual passion.

Johnny told Rose that he could do some shopping for her and would love to share much more about the chemistry of foods and their nutritional properties. From trips into Portland to visit some of his foodie friends, he had already met and learned from some of the best holistic doctors and coaches. They taught him about eating raw foods and how to add 20 years to your life by putting the right foods into your body.

Rose loved their conversations and her deeply spiritual persona shined through as they talked about God's blessings by providing us with amazing foods. They hit it off in a profound way, and it happened instantly.

Their conversations were completely open. Rose even told Johnny that the huge house was

fully paid-off and that she was kind of lonely living in a 9-bedroom house all by herself. And before long, to Johnny's deep pleasure and amazement at how the Wheel of Karma turns, Rose suggested that it seemed fair to do an even trade, and that he would not have to pay anything for living there. He felt a lightness, a wave of freedom, of airy liberation all over his body, both then and every day.

Within no time, Johnny was living in Hollywood, pursuing his mission with a beautiful place to live for FREE and a brand new, loving friend. The two of them prayed together at the end of their conversations and he thanked God for guiding him to the right people, and felt grateful for this beautiful life. He even shed tears and felt them come rushing down his cheeks. Tears of joy.

# CHAPTER 3

## MIKE THE DRUNK

Johnny decided to drive late. It was Friday night, and he was picking people up non-stop. The meter was running wild. At around 2 AM he pulled up to a dive bar right off Sunset Boulevard. Immediately he saw this big guy, and he could see on his app that the big one's name was Mike. He was staggering out of the dive bar walking towards Johnny's car.

Johnny's car windows were down, and he said: "Mike!"

Without stopping, he opened the front door and took the passenger's seat. Johnny had already noticed that 9 out of 10 people immediately jumped in the back without stalling, but he always let them choose to sit anywhere they wanted.

Mike plopped right into the front seat. It was obvious he was very drunk.

He looked at Johnny and slurred out, "Take me to Norms."

Johnny figured that Norms was an all night diner but had never noticed one while driving the streets of Hollywood or LA.

So he just sluffed it off and said, "Sounds great Mike, but you didn't punch an address into the app. So where is Norms?"

When a driver picks people up, most people provide their drop off location. You never know where a pickup is going until they get in your vehicle and you swipe the app. Once in a while, people don't know their drop off address and they just tell the driver how to get to the location. At the end of the ride, the driver swipes the app, and it picks up the location so the driver can get paid.

Mike did not put in an address and when Johnny asked him, he looked around and said, "Take me to Norms," again.

Johnny had tuned into how tanked on booze Mike was and warmed up to him so they wouldn't start to argue. He had learned from being with his uncle that you never want to argue with a damn drunk man.

Johnny said, "No problem, Mike, but you gotta tell me where Norms is located and I will be happy to drive your there."

Mike swayed on the seat, cocked his head, looked out the passenger window, then jerked back to look at Johnny. Squinting one eye, he sized Johnny up and down. His head rocked back. He squinted both eyes and stared hard.

Mike looked at Johnny for a long time then screamed, "Just fucking take me to Norms!!!"

And again Johnny said, "It's all good, Mike, but where is Norms?"

Johnny didn't have a clue which way he had to go to get to Norms and there was no way that he would start driving in the madhouse traffic on Sunset Boulevard while wondering which way to go.

Johnny noticed that Mike's hands were balling up tighter and tighter as fists till his knuckles started turning white, and his face had gotten really red, and he started yelling straight at Johnny with spit coming out of his mouth.

"JUST FUCKING DRIVE!" came slurping out of his mouth as he pushed Johnny's shoulder with his big, meaty left hand and slammed that huge ham hock of a right on Johnny's dashboard.

He yelled again, "You fucking idiot. Drive this dammed rice burner."

Johnny's mom told him over and over again,

from a very young age, that what people said was always a reflection of who they were on the inside. You could see it if you stood at a distance and watched the bullies at school; they had so much pain inside of them that their faces scrunched as they preyed on the weaker kids, spilling all their own garbage out on them.

Johnny could see that, though he was young in years, Mike was already an old man from all of the pain he endured inside. But it didn't really matter, he was still a bully, and probably bullied his wife or kids and friends around. Johnny did notice a wedding ring on his left hand.

Calmly, Johnny lifted his iPhone from the dash, opened his door and got out of the car and said, "Mike, get the fuck out of my car," in a deep, powerful voice.

Mike sat in the car still, but Johnny could feel his loud, drunken energy backing down, and he could see Mike looking at him closely.

Johnny stood there on the asphalt in his jeans and white T-shirt and he could feel his own rugged, country boy confidence in his own power. He also felt the thing he always knew, that being a truly spiritual person made a person authentic in every action. Johnny had always felt sorry for the new age spiritual people who ran around acting so holy and spiritual, but deep inside were spiritual wimps.

His uncle taught him early on to always walk away from trouble and have compassion for people, but his mom made it clear that there are times to be authentic and be real and control your emotions and stay in the moment.

"Get the fuck out of my car Mike." This time it roared out of Johnny's chest like Thor bellowing.

Mike started bellowing really loud. "I spend $500 a month on this service and here you are so fucking dumb you can't find Norms. You're not a DRIVER. YOU are a goddamned imposter. Every DRIVER in The City of Angels knows the fucking Norms locations like the palm of his hand."

"What the fuck do you think you are? You're a complete idiot. Where the hell do you think all the drunks go after the bar? To Juniors or something? Forget about it. Everybody knows you go to Norms for steak and eggs. That's it, motherfucker," said Mike for his closing argument as he stepped back out into the night.

As he had grown louder in his insulted rage, calling Johnny all kinds of names, Johnny noticed a few bouncers at the door of the dive bar. They saw what was going on and came walking over.

A great big guy with a very deep, booming voice said, "Mike, are you causing everybody grief and aggravation again?"

Obviously, Mike was an old standby. He turned to them and boomed out at the top of his lungs. "Get the fuck back, boys. Screw both of you and this stupid ass driver."

The big bouncer said, "Calm down Mike" and walked towards him.

Mike shouted and then pushed a huge black bouncer. Fast as lightning, the big black bouncer guy hit him with a right hook as smooth as Mike Tyson. Bully Mike's lights went out as he fell straight away onto the asphalt.

One of the other bouncers, a tall, lanky white boy with long hair, jumped on bully Mike like a UFC fighter and grabbed him with a chokehold. Johnny watched transfixed as lots of blood came gushing out of Mike's nose and his eyes rolled back in his head.

Johnny walked over to the bouncers.

"Thanks guys," he said.

"Take care of Mike, will you? I think the poor guy was just dying for a steak, and maybe a bowl of menudo at Norms, and I didn't know how to help him out, so he got a little impatient."

They all cracked up and shook Johnny's hand.

"Damn dude, it would sure make our job easier if everybody had an attitude like yours," said the huge black guy.

Johnny looked right in his eyes, "It's all good, dude," he said.

The guy shook Johnny's hand again and said with a big grin, "You got that right, my brother. You got that right for sure."

And Johnny slipped into his ride so he could DRIVE.

## CHAPTER 4

## RITA, RITA GET OUT OF THE GUTTER

The next morning, Johnny was on the road early because it was what ride-sharing companies called surge time, a period of the day when DRIVERS get paid more money because rides are in high demand. He turned on the app; it beeped right away, and at the same time it started pouring rain.

He checked the app screen and it read that he was picking up a woman named Rita who was located 9 minutes away. Johnny headed out and noticed that he needed gas so he stopped at a gas station and decided to pump a few dollars into the tank. He sure didn't want to run out of gas, and at the same time his new fare, Rita, was waiting for him.

Johnny drove up to the gas station, hopped out, slid his card through the pump and grabbed the nozzle, moving as fast as he could go. He stopped with $5 in the tank to speed things up, hopped back in his car and zipped out toward Rita. As all this frantic energy exploded, the rain started thudding down harder and harder and even faster and faster than it had been, until it was next to impossible to see the road. He looked at the app and it appeared that Rita was standing on a business corner. Johnny thought that she might be right there at a bus station, but the app was saying she was 700 feet away. So he stepped on the gas to try to find her.

Suddenly, Johnny heard a big, loud voice yelling and looked in his mirror and he could see a mountain of a woman perched very determinedly right in the middle of the street. Rita was waving her hands like she was going to direct the landing of a supersonic jet on an aircraft carrier, and she was dressed impeccably in a woman's business suit.

Johnny strained to see through the rain that was like a blanket, and slid into the side of the road because now there was a stream of cars behind him, all trying to see with all their might. He wanted to make a fast U-turn but there was just too much going on, and a big divider sat out there in the middle of the boulevard. But through it all, he could see Rita running towards the car in 5-inch heels. Johnny just sat there on the side of the road with his hazard lights on and waited for her.

Rita starting running faster and faster like a full back in an NFL football game. It was now raining cats and dogs. Johnny was still watching her in his mirror, and she was getting closer to the car, but all of a sudden she lost her balance, and she fell flat into the gutter—like she was going

over the football goal line to score and smack, there she was, sliding in the gutter.

Johnny felt frozen, not sure what to do in a situation like this. Suddenly, he jumped out of the car and shot off fast to help her.

He ran hard, right over to her and held out his hand and shouted, "Rita are you OK?"

She was prone in a foot of gutter water, and it seemed as if she might drown. The rain kept getting heavier and thicker and it was coming down fast on both of them.

Rita's lipstick and makeup were smeared all over her face. She looked at Johnny from her position lying in the gutter, and out of nowhere, she started to laugh. Then the huge, weird, boisterous laugh turned into a cry; a loud, mournful wail.

Johnny said, "Rita, here. Take my hand. We need to get you out of the gutter."

She turned slowly, with a great deal of effort, and inched onto her side, and then got to her hands and knees, and then she took Johnny's hand. He tugged to help her up, which required a huge effort from Johnny because she must of weighed 350 pounds or so.

He had to use all of his strength to pull her up. He could see the cars whizzing past looking at them out of the corner of his eye. Rita strained to get up on her feet with a half embarrassed smile. She kind of looked like a circus clown Johnny had seen at a recent performance with his mom where the makeup was such a mess.

They slowly walked backed to the car that was still running with the hazard lights on, and Johnny opened the back door for Rita. He told her he would just turn off the app and take her anywhere she wanted and not charge her for the ride. She asked him to take her back home because she was going to a job interview at Denny's and that she did not want the stupid job in the first place. They did not say much to each other, but he told her that things would work out for the best and tried to give her all the positive energy he could. He knew she was not badly hurt, just thoroughly shaken up.

They got to her place, and he dropped her off. Johnny stayed in the car and watched Rita walk back into her apartment complex. He pulled away and headed to a Starbucks that he had seen a mile away while driving her home. He crawled through the rain into Starbucks to wash up and get some hot green tea.

"Maybe it would be a good time to focus on my new acting class starting at 3 p.m.," he thought, feeling the need to chill all over his body.

The next few months flew by, and Johnny felt clearly that he was making some progress with his acting career. He landed an agent and auditions for a few small parts in movies. His living situation was going well, and Rose the lady that owned the house, was very happy, and she was eating very healthy and was a delight to be around. He felt like she was the grandmother that he never had. He was driving around 5 to 7 hours a day and feeling good that he was bringing in cash flow and that things kept moving forward. His uncle taught him a very useful exercise when he was a teenager. It was called the "Petty Tyrant" exercise that came from the Toltec Indians.

He told Johnny that he should always be working to conserve energy by erasing his ego as much as possible. And one good way to achieve this was to work with bitchy people as if they were Johnny's boss, not fighting them and doing exactly what they said without ever giving in or cow-towing to them.

Deflating the ego should always be one of the main activities in anyone's life. So when people are really bitchy, one should follow their commands, never letting them know what you are doing. This exercise would always bring you back to your real, natural self and wipe away your dependence on your ego. To be honest with you, during Johnny's first rounds of thinking about becoming a DRIVER, the whole idea was really hard because his ego was so bloated.

Johnny always thought that he should be the one with so much money and fame and that he would be the passenger in a big limousine and have his own driver. Becoming a driver, and letting people boss him around really helped Johnny to become more humble. It helped him to learn to listen more, and know that life is about learning to love all people, not self-importance.

Uncle Esposito's exercise really helped Johnny, and he thought that maybe one day when he becomes a multimillionaire, he would drive for FREE just because it is fun.

# CHAPTER 5

## FLYING BULLETS

There were so many different people in Hollywood: the good, the bad, the ugly, the weird, the rich, the poor and on and on and on. Like nowhere else on earth.

It was around 11:30 p.m. on a Thursday night and Johnny had a passenger named Paul. The pick-up location was a place up in the hills with big houses, and it was known as a new money area instead of the old money that was passed down from one generation to the next in Hollywood. He pulled up to the house and there were two guys that looked like they were in their 30's. They were dressed in dark clothes and got into the back seat.

"Hey guys," Johnny said, and they responded, "Hey."

He just drove off and soon realized they did not want to talk. He looked at the app and the destination said 1024 Willow Street, West

Covina, 37 miles away. He had the music on low and just enjoyed the drive. An hour later they came to Willow Street, then on to 1024.

The leader guy, the tougher of the two, the Paul guy, who had really deep brown eyes, said, "Keep on going and pull around the corner."

Right around the corner was an empty parking lot. It looked like a commercial business area. He told Johnny to park there, and then said that if he could manage to wait for them and not take off he would be well rewarded for being their ride back home to Hollywood.

Johnny said, "No problem."

Paul said they would only be a few minutes and got out of the car. They both had sweaters on that had hoods and they put their hoods on at the same time. Johnny turned the car off and sat watching them until they disappeared. The night was very dark, because the moon was not shining, and Johnny was parked near the freeway. The noise of cars created a numbing tunnel of sound; it was a steady roar that drowned out everything else.

He sat around for 10 minutes or so and kept looking into the mirror to see if they were coming. All the sudden he could see Paul and his friend, without his hooded sweater, running toward him. Because he had the window down, he could hear

them say "GO, GO, GO."

He fired up the car, dug into reverse, backed out, then shoved it in drive, clicked on the door's unlock button and started to drive slow, to pull forward.

Paul and his pal were getting closer to the car and Johnny could see two other guys behind them, chasing them, and he heard boom, boom, boom—they were shooting at them.

Paul and his buddy jumped in the back seat yelling, "Get the fuck out of here."

They threw a big black duffle bag into the back seat and again yelled, "GO, GO, GO."

The back doors were still open, and he stepped on the gas. The gunshots were coming at them in the car, slashing right through the back window. Paul's friend turned around and started shooting back, boom, boom, boom. Johnny jammed his foot on the gas even harder. He did not realize how fast his little Toyota could go. He shot out like he was in a car at Daytona.

He felt pretty good about his driving skills and it felt like he was acting in a Hollywood movie, but this was for real. Johnny raced down the street and made it around the corner and could not see the two guys; they were out of sight. He thought they might have jumped into their car and could be still chasing him, so he drove very fast down a few side streets. Johnny then clicked on the app and started heading back to Hollywood. He heard Paul ask his friend if he was OK. The guy said he was fine. Johnny hopped on the 10 West toward Hollywood. He looked in the mirror and the whole back window was completely busted out from gunshots. He turned on the heat a little to keep the car warm.

Paul said, "Don't worry about your window; we will take care of it. Just keep driving and get us home."

Johnny knew it was not the right time to talk, so he just kept driving and thought of the exercise his uncle taught him, about the "Petty Tyrant."

Johnny made Paul and his pal his "Petty Tyrants."

They were full of total bad boy ego as thick as flies on shit.

People like to romanticize crooks as if they had a heart of gold under it all, but they don't. They are petty politicians who use blunt force trauma to enforce their rulings just like politicians use their Nazi police forces to do it for them. It was perfect turf.

These guys were true "Petty Tyrants," used to pushing people around and Johnny knew that, because their tough guy egos were so thick, he could totally fake them out by being completely subservient to their every wish, and not complaining. He would use this perfect timing to drop his ego completely, not feel sorry for himself, and follow their every command as if he were a complete idiot; but they would be confused and thrown off because they would be able to feel underneath how strong he was.

Johnny knew that this episode was a very advanced one in his training, but he knew the night was not over yet. He got off the exit towards their house and pulled into the street were he'd picked them up. He did everything exactly as they said and they were kind of amazed, though they were macho dummies that had learned to hide their feelings.

"Pull into the drive," said the lame partner.

Johnny had noticed there were no cars, so he said, "Which side should I pull into?"

The partner grunted and poked Johnny in the back of the neck with his pistol. Paul opened the garage with his controller and Johnny followed all directions quickly, to the letter, and perfectly. They told him to turn off the engine and they sat quietly in the garage.

Paul unzipped the big black duffel bag and

Johnny watched him in the mirrors. The lame partner jammed the pistol up to the back of Johnny's head again. He could see that Paul was digging into the duffel.

"This guy is kind of a smart ass or something," said the dude, jamming the pistol hard into Johnny's head.

"Let's just take care of him now. Something's funny about him."

"Are you kidding me?" Said Paul.

"He fucking does everything just right, perfectly."

"This motherfucker can turn us in," said the partner.

"No," said Paul, "this motherfucker is now part of our team, so if we go down, he comes with us."

Johnny could see Paul put his hand on the gun and pulled it away from his head. "What is your fucking name, dude?"

"Johnny."

Paul pulled huge bundles of hundred dollar bills up so Johnny could see them in the mirror. It was kind of unbelievable. He tossed two stacks over into Johnny's lap. Each bundle said $10,000 on them. Johnny thought there must be close to a million dollars in the duffel bag.

"How's that, 20 grand for fixing your car, and your pay for being our DRIVER? How about it, Johnny, is it a deal?"

Johnny slowly picked up the money and said, "You've got it. It's all between us and I am your DRIVER now."

Paul closed the duffel, nudged his partner and got out of the car, walked and clicked on a button on the side of the house, and the door slid open. The pair disappeared into the house.

Johnny started up the car and slowly eased down the block amazed. He looked at the two bundles of hundred dollar bills, thought about stopping at a car wash to clean up a bit, but thought it would be a big risk so he decided just to go home.

He drove up the driveway to his beautiful home. His fab new friend, Rose, was probably waiting inside, and Johnny thought he would prepare a wonderful midnight meal. He put one of the stacks of bills on a finger and looked at himself in the mirror.

"We're gonna spin this town," he said, twirling the bundle on the tip of his index finger.

# CHAPTER 6

## INNOCENT UCLA STUDENT

The next few months had Johnny back in the "chop wood, carry water" mode, like the Zen master would say.

He had stumbled into enlightenment. However, when a person becomes enlightened, you just go back to ordinary life, to the same old thing.

Of course it wasn't entirely that way. Johnny WAS in Hollywood pursuing his dream. He had plenty of cash, a great home, and plenty of new friends, but what had changed was that he realized that life was a journey and there was nowhere to get to. Even when he had his big break and became a star, it would all be the same at the ground level. Life was about enjoying each day and each moment.

On a Tuesday morning in the spring, Johnny's agent called and told him that they might have hit

a big break, because there was a solid part, the movie was already financed, and the producer wanted him to do a reading at 2 p.m. He had already seen Johnny in a few videos and thought he might be perfect for the part. Johnny's agent said the producer wanted him to come for a casual meeting at his house by the pool, so he should bring some swimming gear. Right at the end of the conversation, his agent told him that if he got the part it would pay over 2 million and could easily be his entry to Hollywood success.

Johnny hung up the phone and thought he would drive for a few hours to rake in a little cash. He jumped into the shower, got dressed and had a fare waiting up near UCLA. She was a young Chinese girl, probably 22 or so. The app said her name was Fiona. Johnny could tell that she was really shy the minute he saw her, and it was obvious that she was really, really smart.

They started talking, and after he asked her some really personal questions, they broke into a long, exciting conversation. He even threw in a few words of Chinese, simple things he had picked up from some Chinese acting friends.

Fiona was really impressed that an American actually knew a little taste of Chinese. Johnny had always been fascinated with Asian culture, especially the healing energy parts like Acuputure, Chigong, Taoism, and especially Tantra. Their conversation bubbled over, and he could feel that she took a shine to him. He asked her who she lived with, and she told him that she lived alone, and explained that she had a small balcony area where she grew a lot of healing herbs that her grandmother used to grow in China.

Fiona said that her family always believed in healing herbs and energy work, and asked Johnny if he wanted to see her herb garden. He was happy that she wanted to get to know him better, and he sensed that she felt a little homesick and lonely. He could feel it. So, he accepted her invitation and pulled into her apartment complex and she told him that he could park in her car spot. She laughed, and said that she did not even own a car and was happy that they could put the empty carport to use. They got out of the car. She was wearing a short, cute schoolgirl skirt, and Johnny could tell she had a really nice sexy petite body. Fiona started to giggle and told him that she had never brought a man to her place before.

She carried her heavy book bag, and he took it from her, saying, "Here, let me help."

The gesture of kindness made her feel really warm toward Johnny. He could instantly see how happy it made her. As her front door opened he could see a shoe rack, so he took off his shoes. Her apartment was very simple and very messy.

She got a little embarrassed and said she was not planning to invite anyone over, "Sorry my place is so messy."

She started to pick up some cloths and grabbed a bath towel and put it away.

Johnny asked if he could use her rest room and as he came out he heard her boiling water. She asked if he would like some tea. Fiona had two cups already out and poured the tea. She turned to him and said, "I will be back. Let the tea cool down."

She took a long time in the rest room, and when she came out, she wore lipstick and had let her hair down. It was wonderful, thick, so long and jet-black and her eyes were penetrating and her lips magnetic.

She took the cooled cup of tea, handing the other to Johnny and they sat calmly sipping. While they talked, they touched hands a few times, and her milky Asian skin was like a magnet.

He knew deep in her unconscious mind she desired a man. He could always recognize when a woman desired him, and especially when he desired her. They never even talked about her herb garden. He thought about asking her, but knew that it was no longer important.

For a number of years Johnny had studied Tantra and was an expert in how to bring the beautiful feminine Goddess out of a woman. He knew that all women wanted to be desired, and to be sexually craved by a man, and that women highly desire to be ravished by a man, by any man or even by their own man. He always loved the word "ravished" and the meaning of the word.

Fiona was sitting across from him, and he noticed that he could see her white panties as she stood to get them more tea. He felt himself get a little aroused. Johnny knew that they had a deep connection or good chemistry, or potential love at first sight.

He could feel how they both wanted each other. For him, after he got Tantra training, he never wanted to just have sex with a woman for simply bodily pleasure. He always desired a mind and spiritual connection along with the physical. For him sex had become spiritual and healing and much more rich and meaningful. A true sexual-spiritual relationship is about the conversation and the spirit, and then sex becomes a beautiful, special event between two people.

The chairs they were sitting on seemed to

move closer on their own, and their legs were pressing slightly against each other. Johnny could feel a magnetic charge that they had with each other. He noticed her firm breasts and could see her cleavage. He put his hand on top of her hand and felt how soft her skin was and felt how sweet and giving this girl was.

She squeezed his biceps and said, "You have such a strong body Johnny, and you are so tall."

He stood up and said, "Let's see how tall you are."

She stood up and then he pulled her closer into his arms and hugged her. He could feel her body melt into his body, and they had this electrical charge going through their entire bodies.

He slowly bent down and kissed her neck, and he could see goose bumps on her neck and arms. Johnny kissed her neck gently and slowly moved his mouth down onto her chest area and began kissed her cleavage and the top of each firm breast. She made noises like she was already feeling really good.

Johnny then used his hand to lift her breast out of her bra and continued kissing her beautiful body. He then moved his head close to her lips and looked deep into her eyes. He felt himself melting in love, looking deep into her eyes, and her eyes turned into sparkly diamonds.

Then they started to kiss deeply like they had been looking for each other their whole lives, as if they were soul mates yearning for each other.

She moaned even louder. He reached down and put his hand on her soft white underwear, and continued to touched her body. It really turned Johnny on that she was so wet for him.

She then jumped onto him and wrapped her legs around him while he was standing up. She only weighed maybe 107 or so. She was so petite but with nice, big, firm breasts. Then he put his hands on her ass, and it was so firm and round for a small petite Asian girl.

He kept her legs wrapped around him and walked into her bedroom and laid her on the bed and slowing slipped off her panties and used his lips to give her pleasure. She did not hold any thing back and screamed so loudly that he thought her whole apartment complex could hear.

Then Johnny undressed Fiona and told her to stand up so he could look at her, and see how beautiful she was.

He always enjoyed pleasuring women and ravishing them with love because then they would be giving because they felt so much love and pleasure. He saw how beautiful she was inside and out and his heart wanted to pleasure her even more.

Johnny wanted to give her even more pleasure, and then Fiona said, "I want you to make love to me."

He quickly took his clothes off and was ready for her.

She looked at Johnny and felt his love and she also thought he was beautiful too.

Johnny kissed Fiona deeply and thought how much he wanted her.

As Johnny made love to her it was obvious that she enjoyed it very much. He could tell that as she instantly had another orgasm.

Tantra had taught him to control himself so he could release himself in minutes or last for hours. Johnny once read that the rock star Sting was also a Tantra master and had once been reported as having made love to his wife for 8 hours.

Johnny and Fiona made love for hours. After that they lay in each other arms and talked just as deeply as the sex was. Johnny looked at the clock and it was 1 p.m. He told her about his potential big break in getting this key role and his meeting with the Hollywood producer.

Fiona was very positive and told him she had a feeling that he would get the part.

She said, "Go take a shower, get ready, and be on time."

He kissed her forehead and thanked her for sharing herself with him and that he appreciated her very much.

Fiona was really happy and giggled with her cute laugh.

# CHAPTER 7

## A BALL BUSTER DECISION

Johnny got in the car and looked in the back seat to make sure he had his swim trunks with him. He checked the GPS and punched in the producer's address. Shortly thereafter he pulled up to a secure gate with security guards, gave the security attendant his name, and the producer already had him on his list. He drove onto a magnificent home that really looked like it belonged to a film producer.

Johnny knocked on the door and the producer's house servant introduced himself and said, "You must be Johnny."

He explained that Johnny could change into his swimwear and meet the producer by the pool. Johnny went into a luxury bathroom that looked like it belonged in the Ritz Carlton, and changed into his shorts. There was a big fluffy beach towel and a place to keep his clothes so he grabbed the towel and headed out of the restroom, and the butler walked him out to the pool area.

He looked and could see the producer, who said, "Johnny."

He knew what the producer looked like because he had looked him up online. The producer was in his late 50's and had many, many years of great success making #1 box office hit movies. He was sipping a martini and asked Johnny if he wanted one. Johnny did not drink very often and really did not like alcohol but felt that he should accept. They drank a few martinis and swam in the pool and had a pretty fun time. He was a nice guy, but Johnny's intuitive voice picked up that the guy liked men. Johnny had nothing against gay men or women; he was just sure that he really enjoyed women and had no sexual desire for other men. He heard about a lot of actors doing whatever it took to get what they wanted in Hollywood, and actually, he used to joke around after acting class with his classmates about whether they would you perform a sexual act to get a big million dollar part in a movie.

Most of the actors would say, "Hell yea, I would for sure." A few would say they were not so sure they would.

The producer asked if he wanted to sit in the Jacuzzi and explained that he had no chlorine in the pool or Jacuzzi. He explained that the Jacuzzi had hydrogen peroxide in it, and that the chlorine in our water system was slowly killing all of us.

The producer said that it was especially keeping us slow and dumb, trapping us, and dumping us into the matrix. Johnny agreed completely and told him that he had a filter on his shower at home.

They headed to the Jacuzzi and the producer slowly took off his shorts and said there was no swimwear allowed in the Jacuzzi. Johnny took off his shorts too. He did not mind because he occasionally went to a Korean spa and there they

have the same rules.

They sat in the Jacuzzi and it felt really good because the day was kind of cloudy, and the sun went behind a few clouds and it got a bit chilly. They started talking about the part in the movie and he told Johnny to tell him why he should choose him for it. He asked a lot of questions, and Johnny just answered him with his true passion about life and his purpose for his acting career. He knew that the most power a man could have was always to be authentic and to simply relax and be people's friends in a conversation.

They got more and more involved in a really good conversation for about an hour or so. He then told Johnny that he had a few more male actors that he thought might be good for the part in the movie. The producer told Johnny that he liked to get to know a potential actor in a setting like this. He then stood up in the Jacuzzi and sat on the concrete edge, with his feet dangled in the water.

He asked Johnny to show him how determined he was to get the part, and he kind of opened his legs a bit wider and put his hand on his cock. Johnny could see that he was getting a hard on. Then, again, he asked Johnny to show him that he really wanted the part, and that if he did want the part, he would not even meet the other two actors. He said that Johnny would get his Hollywood break, and he would make him a star. Johnny looked again, and the guy was completely hard, and his dick stood straight up.

Johnny looked up to the sky and saw a few puffy clouds and the sun was getting ready to come out from behind the clouds and his mind wondered off. He started to think about his new taxi job, about being THE DRIVER. His mind flashed back to Rita in the gutter looking like a circus clown, and then his mind flashed to the two guys that put a gun to his head and the leader throwing the money in his lap, telling him, "You are our DRIVER."

Mike the bully floated through his mind, and how the bouncers kicked his ass. Johnny smiled, and the sun broke out of the clouds and started shinning on his face. He stood up in the Jacuzzi and looked at the producer again.

The guy had a big smile on his face, and holding his hard penis in his hand, he said, "Show me you are the man for the part, Johnny."

Johnny knew he had a ball buster decision to make in the next 2 seconds.

Johnny looked at the producer and said, "Let's get real here. Looking at you does not do anything for me, nothing at all. I have nothing against gay people or bisexual people or whatever your preference is. If it turned me on to look at you I would not have a problem, but the truth is I really enjoy women a lot and I would never do anything in this lifetime unless it was honest. I know I have the looks to be a great actor and also I have the dedication and I know how to be authentic on camera, therefore, if you are going to give me, or anyone, the part in your movie because of a favor, then screw you. I don't want to be in your movie. I am dedicated to working hard and to be the best I can be in your movie and if that's not good enough, another part will come to me."

Then Johnny stepped back and got out of the Jacuzzi, grabbed a towel, and said, "Thank you for your time."

He did not even look back, and the producer did not say a word. Johnny always felt a man has his true power when he can walk away from anything. Walk away from a bad relationship or walk away from money. He felt that when you become desperate for something in life that is exactly the time when people will walk on you and take advantage of you. He felt good about his decision and walked away feeling very powerful in his energy. Johnny went into the producer's house, changed into his clothes, and headed for his car.

He started up the engine and looked in the mirror and saw his big blue eyes and said, "Good job, driver."

# CHAPTER 8

## RAY THE NET WORKER

Johnny drove into LAX and was looking for Southwest Airlines to pick up a guy named Ray. He pulled over to the curb and saw a good-looking man wave his hand. On the app, the rider knows the color, year, and make of the vehicle, so Johnny assumed it was Ray.

Johnny got out and helped Ray with his luggage and put it into the car. Johnny got back into the car and looked at the app; Ray was going to the Ritz Carlton in Laguna Beach.

Johnny said to Ray, "Hi, it looks like you're heading to Laguna Beach."

Ray responded, "Yes, that's where I'm headed, to attend the Millionaire Club for my networking company."

His company was a billion-dollar company—one of the top performers in the field. He started talking about how he had hundreds of thousands of people in his "downline."

Johnny had a few friends in network marketing so he understood the concept very well.

Ray asked Johnny if he had ever considered making money off of other people's efforts, and told him that network marketing was a great way to build a team and make an immense amount of money. Johnny said that he agreed with that concept 100%, and that he has learned to stay focused on one thing at a time. Johnny said that he took a driving job to see California and make a little cashflow to pay the bills, but he was only focused on being a great actor and landing a lead in a major block buster movie in Hollywood.

Ray agreed on staying focused and told Johnny that this is what he teaches his downline. Ray continued to explain that he got lucky and found one company that he has been working with and built this huge downline and created great systems to duplicate. His managers then quickly put money into a new distributor.

Ray said this was why he became so wealthy in the industry; most people never really teach the new distributor to put money into his pocket fast while continuing to make more and more money each month so they can eventually quit their jobs.

Ray asked Johnny for his phone number and told him that when he gets his big break in his movie, he would let his whole downline know about the movie. Johnny thought this was a good way to market something when you have thousands of loyal fans or customers. He had met some people that spent tons of money either on inventing a product or writing a book, but they never made any money because they only had a few friends and the product never got out to the masses.

Johnny thought Ray was a really cool and focused guy; he had a feeling that Ray was a person that he wanted to stay in touch with. He was an action guy instead of just talking about making things happen.

Johnny's GPS lead him to 133 Laguna Canyon Road. Ray told Johnny to roll down all the windows and feel the fresh air.

Johnny's windows were down and Ray stuck his head out his window and started to yell, "Life is good, life is good."

Johnny started to yell too; "Life is good."

They could see the ocean and main beach on the Pacific Coast Highway. The ocean looked so beautiful. They headed south on PCH towards the Ritz Carton. Johnny and Ray both continued to yell out of the window and laugh. Johnny felt so alive and free and in the moment. He began to yell, "Be here now."

He thought of his uncle, who always told him that being in a struggle is when your mind is projecting into the future or thinking about the past. If your mind is in the moment, then all is good.

Johnny pulled up to the Ritz Carlton. Ray shook Johnny's hand and told him, "God Bless," and tipped him a $20 bill and said he would be in touch.

Johnny thanked Ray and told him they should stay in touch and that he would invite him to his first big movie release.

Ray looked Johnny in the eye and said, "I have no doubt that you will be a Hollywood star."

Johnny watched as Ray walked into the Ritz and then looked at the $20 bill, and realized that more and more people were tipping him. He always appreciated the tips because it paid for his gas money.

When ride-sharing companies started up they got more riders because they told people that they did not need to tip and it would be cheaper for the rider. Now it is starting to change and more and more people want to tip because it is a lot better experience for the rider.

Johnny did a few more pick-ups and then headed back to Hollywood feeling alive and loving life.

# CHAPTER 9

## PISSED OFF TAXI DRIVERS

Johnny looked at his Driver's app and he was picking up a rider at LAX. He just finished taking an easy exam online to be able to pick up riders from there.

If you get caught picking up a rider at the airport and you did not take the Driver's exam you can get a substantial fine from the airport police. In LA the taxi cab drivers really hate all the ride-sharing companies. In fact not only in LA but just about every big city in the world.

The night before, Johnny was looking at some YouTube videos. He watched one of a taxi guy in Canada going crazy, yelling at a ride-sharing driver. He told him that he had no experience being a driver and how he was a fake and did not know what he was doing and was unprofessional. He started to bang on the driver's window, almost breaking it. Then the driver took off and the taxi guy jumped on the driver's car, hanging on while the car drove down the street. Luckily the taxi guy did not kill himself.

Another video, that Johnny watched, showed the taxi guys on strike and very mad that their jobs are being taken away by the ride-sharing companies that are getting more and more business. A video from Australia shows the taxi guy so mad at a ride-share driver that he looks like he wants to kill him. The taxi guy accuses him of not having the qualifications to be a driver. The ride-share driver kept on telling the taxi guy that all you need is a valid driver's license; then you pick up a rider and follow your GPS. The taxi guy told the driver that he was not educated enough to drive. The driver told the taxi guy that he was working on his PhD, and this was the reason he was driving—to pay his way through school. At this point, the taxi guy looked like he wanted to kill him, and he started to kick and hit his car as the driver sped off.

Most people Johnny picked up were really happy that a handsome guy in a very clean car and great personality picked them up. People were grateful not to be in a stinky taxicab being charged an arm and leg just to go across town. A few of his customers talked about how most taxicab companies were owned either by big corporations or very bad people that had monopolized the industry for many years. They had no customer service standards and charged very high prices. The people were glad that they had a choice now. Customers told Johnny that even Apple is getting into the business and had just invested $1 billion in the largest ride sharing company in China called Didi Chuxing. Big companies were now buying up ride-sharing companies and car companies are getting involved.

Johnny realized that life was always about constant change. He had a feeling that one-day taxicabs would no longer be on the streets; kind of like the way Blockbuster Video stores went out of business.

Change will happen with or without you, and whether you like it or not. Johnny always kept in mind that living a good life was about non-judgment, non-resistance and non-attachment; he was always working on all three of these approaches and he constantly reminded himself of them.

# CHAPTER 10

# THE CALL GIRL

On a Friday night around 9:30 p.m., Johnny picked up a rider named Stephanie. He pulled up to an apartment complex and waited for her. He saw this really tall girl walking towards him. She was in 4-inch heels that made her at least 6ft or more; she was wearing a black mini skirt and a blouse that made her breasts bulge out. This girl was blessed with a body that any man would die for.

Stephanie came to the front seat and asked, "Can I sit there."

Johnny said, "sure," and she sat down.

Johnny could tell that this girl was maybe 18 or 19 years old and she was very nervous. Johnny was good at making people feel comfortable around him. He looked at his cell phone and said to Stephanie that it looked like she is going to

Beverly Hills. He put the car in drive and slowly started on the trip.

Johnny said, "You look very elegant tonight—are you going to a party?"

The young girl said, "Not really, I am kinda going to work."

Johnny responded, "Ohh…"

He felt her energy becoming very nervous again but it seemed like she wanted to talk. From driving all kinds of people in this crazy city called Hollywood, Johnny got pretty good at knowing about his customers. Johnny had a pretty good idea as to what type of work Stephanie did by the way she was dressed. He knew the area in Beverly Hills that he was taking her to, where there are only multi-million dollar houses and many divorced old men looking for some entertainment and pleasure on a Friday night.

"How do you like being a driver?" Stephanie asked.

Johnny started laughing. "I certainly live a more exciting life as a driver than I used to. I get to meet all kinds of people from different walks of life and styles. It is the perfect job for me to bring in cash flow to pay the bills. But, it's only a temporary job to help me reach my true desires and goals."

Stephanie asked Johnny, "What are your real goals?"

Johnny stopped at a red light and looked at her. She had these big brown eyes that he looked straight into and said, "I am going to be the best actor and land a major role in a Hollywood blockbuster movie."

Stephanie looked back at him. "Wow—I see it—and...yeah, I can see that happening because you have so much confidence."

Johnny started to feel emotional, like his eyes were going to tear; it was as though he was dreaming, sitting there with a beautiful girl at a red light in Hollywood. He knew that all of his goals would come to true as long as he worked hard and stayed focused. Somehow Johnny had the knowledge that he could create anything he wanted in life.

Johnny then asked Stephanie the same question: "What are your dreams?"

Stephanie paused for a moment and said, "I don't know. I moved out here six months ago with my boyfriend—now my ex-boyfriend. I just want to stay here and make some money so I don't have to go back home. My mom is a raging alcoholic and my step-father is a frickin' bastard."

Johnny noticed the look on Stephanie's face when she said this. It was clear that her stepfather took advantage of her in some way. He asked her why she broke up with her boyfriend.

"He was overly possessive and jealous," Stephanie said. "I felt like I was in prison. If I so much as looked in the direction of another guy, he would start a fight with me. He would also start fights with other guys for no reason. I just couldn't stand it."

"Who are you living with now?" Johnny asked.

"I'm staying with a girl that I met in yoga class. She was the one who told me that I would be perfect for my new job."

Johnny asked Stephanie if she liked her new job. She looked like she was going to start crying, so Johnny said, "You don't need to tell me—it's OK."

Stephanie responded. "I've learned quickly to turn myself off emotionally. Maybe I should become an actor; after all what I'm doing is pretty much acting. Most of the men are old and they're all rich. They like it when I act a certain way for them. You know—like making believe I'm a schoolgirl or a secretary. As I said, it's like acting. I often get drunk to just numb myself."

Johnny started to feel really bad for her because he could see that she was really emotionally weak and not very strong underneath her beauty.

"My roommate is making good money in porn, and I might try to look into it too," Stephanie said.

Johnny just listened and tried to not give any advice. He realized that sometimes he was better off just listening and if someone needed advice, they would ask for it. There are some people who give so much advice because they just want to hear their own voice. You tell some people about your vacation or something really good and then in the middle they would steal the thunder and tell you all about their vacation or about the subject you are talking about. Johnny always felt that listening is what people really wanted. And when you ask more questions people continue to open up and talk about real stuff, and when you do talk, you share your real stuff and people will trust you more.

Johnny looked at his cell phone and the app said they were almost at Stephanie's destination.

She said to Johnny, "I bet you really look down on me, don't you?"

Johnny slowed down because the app said

400 feet away from the destination.

Johnny said, "I don't judge you, and only wish you the best."

He then pulled up to the big house and said, "We are here."

She straightened up in her seat. Johnny could tell that she turned off all of her openness.

Stephanie said, "Thanks for the ride," and walked up to the house.

He could see the front door open and an old gray-haired man appeared from the light on the front porch. She disappeared into the house.

# CHAPTER 11

# ACTING CLASS

When Johnny was in school, he didn't understand why he had to shine in all of his subjects if he didn't like them. He did have a really good memory and remembered most of the crap that he learned. He always liked group projects that people could work on as a team, instead of trying to be good at everything. With his good looks and size, Johnny was just a natural leader; he knew how to put a team together and bring out the best in each team player.

He enrolled into acting school and one class would lead to another. He was going to school just about every day, and he really loved it and wanted to learn from the best. Johnny felt so natural at it and had this burning desire to reach the top.

In class they had to do a lot of role-playing and acting scenes. The key with acting is you need to become the part you're portraying and make it seem like you're not even acting at all.

They had to watch many movies with some of the best actors and see how real they were on camera. Some people couldn't pull it off; you could tell right away that they were acting for the camera. Johnny never had that problem—he always immersed himself in the part that he was playing.

Acting school is where Johnny finally flourished; he was like the A students in school where academics just came easy for them. That is how Johnny felt; it was just easy for him. He loved that feeling.

Johnny liked to read a lot about Taoism and Tantra and to get into the flow of things and be in the moment. When it came to acting Johnny always felt like he was in flow; it felt effortless. He never really tried—it would just happen for him.

In one acting class the teacher called him up to the front of the class with another guy. The teacher told Johnny that he needed to act as though the other guy, playing his best friend, stole his watch. His objective was to get it back from the other student, who in turn needed to act as though he didn't steal the watch and wouldn't give it back. Johnny got so much into the part that the teacher had to break up Johnny and the other

student. It turned into a real fight and Johnny did get the watch back and almost beat the hell out of the other student. He felt a little bad and apologized to the other student and told him that he was sorry. Johnny could tell the other student thought Johnny was very intense and could feel his power.

He applied himself completely to each and every class. His teachers constantly told Johnny that he had a raw talent and said he would do extremely well if he kept focused. That is why Johnny did not mind being a driver because he had time to himself, and when he picked up riders he could practice being real and authentic, because that was what a true actor did on camera.

His teacher taught Johnny that for each part they were playing they had to understand the true emotions and feelings of the character. The teacher explained that some actors took it to extremes, like in the case of one actor who played a guy that got hooked on drugs and alcohol. The actor really experienced drugs and alcohol and lost almost 50 pounds for the part; he "became" the role he was playing.

Johnny really got that about acting and that is what he liked the best. He realized that to become known in Hollywood you must be a great actor and it was all about what people you know. Johnny got the best agents and teachers so they would put him in direct contact with the people that could make him a true Hollywood actor. Johnny completely dedicated himself 100% to acting and he would do whatever it took to succeed at his mission and purpose in life.

Johnny hung out with friends occasionally, but he only wanted to stay laser-focused on acting and spend as much time as possible becoming the best.

# CHAPTER 12

## PAT: IS IT A MAN OR A WOMAN?

It was Sunday evening and Johnny was getting pretty tired, but he told himself that he would do one more ride and then call it a night.

His app "dinged" and it said he needed to pick up a person called Pat. Johnny kinda laughed to himself, because he remembered watching the TV show Saturday Night Live as a young kid where they had a skit called, "It's Pat." The character named Pat was so ambiguous that you couldn't tell if it was a man or a woman. The other characters always tried to ask questions to figure out if Pat was a man or woman but Pat always answered all the questions they asked so vaguely that the responses could go both ways. It was pretty funny because they could never figure out if Pat was a man or a woman.

Pat would say, "I am going on a date tonight."

The other characters in the skit would ask, "Who are you going out with Pat?" hoping to finally learn the truth.

But then Pat would say, "I am going out at 7 pm and Gene/Jean is picking me up."

Of course, the name "Gene/Jean" can be either a man or a woman. Johnny remembered that his uncle would laugh really hard and that made Johnny laugh too.

Johnny pulled up to an apartment complex in Hollywood, and looked at his phone. It was 1:15 am. He drove to the apartment building's gate and waited there for Pat.

In the distance, he saw an overweight lady dressed in high heels who was slowly approaching his vehicle. Pat came up to the car and opened the front door and plopped into the front seat.

Johnny had a book and a few papers on the front seat and he had to quickly move them because Pat would have sat right on top of everything. Johnny purposefully put a few things on the front seat because he really preferred the riders to sit in the back seat unless it was a pretty girl or cool guy.

When Pat sat in the front seat, Johnny noticed Pat's black dress with panty hose, and the left leg had a big tear running down it. Pat had a big

white pearl necklace with these big fish snap-on earrings.

Johnny studied Pat's face because the interior car light was still on, making it light up like a spot light was on it. Pat's makeup was really thick and her black grayish hair was coming out. Pat's eyeliner was smeared on the side of her face.

Johnny thought of how he was just thinking of the Saturday Night Live skit and of what his acting teacher said: "You are what you think, and we are almost manifesting life all the time."

Johnny said, "Hi Pat, it looks like you are heading south towards Santa Monica." Johnny knew this because the app told him so.

Pat looked at Johnny and said, "Yes darling," in a deep voice that sort of sounded like a woman that had become harsh from excessive smoking.

A phone started to ring, and Pat started looking through a big black purse and found the phone and talked in the same harsh voice. Pat kept on calling the other person on the line darling; "Yes darling I am on my way."

Johnny could hear that it was a man's voice on the other end. Pat continued to talk on the phone and then started to yell at the person on the other end, but continued to say "darling" in responding to him.

Then Pat hung up the phone and leaned somewhat close to Johnny and said, "Darling, do you think we can find a 7-Eleven or a 24-hour liquor store? I need to get some Jack Daniels, and I'll be happy to buy you something too or give you a big tip darling."

Johnny said he would keep his eye out for an open store. Pat thanked Johnny, and he then asked, "Are you going to see a friend?"

Pat replied, "Yes darling, I just met someone and it is kind of special so far and he asked me over for a late night drink, or I should say an early morning drink. He might end up like all the douche bags that I have dated but you never know until you try. You know what I am saying Darling?"

Right then Johnny saw a liquor store that had a big "Open 24 Hours" sign on it. Johnny pulled into it and parked his car. Pat looked at Johnny with her eye liner eyes and bright red lipstick and said, "Do you think you can go in and buy me the biggest bottle of JD they have?"

Pat started reaching into her big black purse and pulled out a crisp hundred-dollar bill and handed it to Johnny. Johnny took the money and went into the store. He walked in and a nice looking older Indian man was working the store and asked Johnny how could he help him.

Johnny got a bottle of Jack Daniels, paid for it and walked back to the car. He slowly opened the door and Pat's head was leaning to the side and was sound asleep. Johnny shut the door and Pat made a little yelling sound and opened her eyes as if from a bad dream. It slightly frightened Johnny how she looked.

Johnny handed her a brown paper sack and said, "Pat, I got your JD, and your change is in the bag."

Pat took the bottle and opened it immediately and started to chug the bottle down. After the big 10-second drink, Pat let out a big burp and said, "That is good shit darling, do you want a drink?"

Johnny declined, explaining that he needed to stay alert and drive. Pat reached into the bag and pulled out a $20 bill, thanked Johnny and handed it to him.

Johnny said, "No that's OK," but Pat put it in his hand, adding, "You're a darling sweet boy."

Johnny thanked her and put the bill in his front pocket. He pulled out of the parking lot and made a left hand turn, and right away Johnny noticed red flashing lights in his rear view mirror. Johnny told Pat that they were getting pulled over by the cops. Johnny pulled over to the side of the road and turned off his engine.

A cop walked up to Johnny's door and said, "Good morning, can I see your driver's license, registration, and insurance, please?"

Johnny slowly reached into his back pocket and took out his driver's license, and then grabbed the registration and insurance card from the glove compartment. He handed it both of them to the police officer. His car smelled like it was a bar on Sunset Boulevard from Pat's big bottle of Jack Daniels.

Johnny asked the policeman politely, "Did I do something wrong, officer?" The cop explained that Johnny had crossed two yellow lines and made an illegal turn out of the liquor store's parking lot.

"Really? It looked like it was a broken yellow line when I turned out into the lane."

Then the officer shined his flashlight in Johnny's eyes and asked, "Have you and your girlfriend been drinking?"

The officer went on to shine the flashlight in Pat's eyes. "Hi darling," was Pat's response to the police officer, complete with the thick make up and smeared eyeliner, bright red lipstick, and a sideways smile.

Johnny was worried how this must look so

he made sure that he told the officer that he was working as a Driver and that Pat requested to stop and get a bottle of Jack Daniels. He was just driving Pat to her destination. The cop shined the light in Johnny's face again and on the car dashboard and saw the emblem of the ride sharing company. The cop looked at Johnny again and handed his license and stuff back to him and said, "Drive safe and have a nice night."

Johnny's heart was pounding because he knew that cops could be pretty authoritative most of the time; he felt lucky that the cop did not give him a ticket and also did not say anything about Pat smelling like a brewery.

Pat's phone started ringing again. Pat answered the phone, but this time forgot to put a woman's voice on and sounded more like a man, and said, "We just got pulled over by the cops darling, and this sweet driver talked his way out of a ticket. Hold your horses we are on our way."

Pat hung up the phone and started to pound the JD down, like it was lemonade on a hot day. Johnny looked in his mirror and hoped the cop did not see this; he didn't want to get a ticket for an open container in his vehicle. He started his engine, turned on his blinker and got back driving to Pat's destination.

"You are a sweet talker," Pat slurred, before starting at the JD again.

Johnny just kept focused on the road and felt very alert and awake. In the next few minutes, Pat's head started to lean towards Johnny because she was falling asleep, and then would abruptly wake up and just stare at Johnny like she did not know where she was or who she was.

Johnny could feel Pat intensely looking even when he was focused on driving. Pat would fall back to sleep and every few minutes start staring again, without any signs of lucidity. Johnny felt like he was dreaming; he felt light-headed and was getting pretty tired. That stare was so intense—like she was going to kill him or something. Johnny finally got to Pat's destination and pulled up to the address on the app.

Johnny said, "Pat, wake up—we are here," and once again, she jumped and started staring at Johnny in a really weird way.

Johnny repeated, "Pat, we are here," but Pat just kept staring at him.

Seemingly, out of the trance, Pat grabbed the bottle of JD and took a big drink followed by, "Thank you for the ride, darling."

Pat grabbed the purse and put the bottle in it, took out a handful of money and handed it to Johnny. Then Pat opened the car door and stumbled out in her high heels.

Johnny let out a long sigh of relief, clicked the app, turned it off, and thought about his nice bed and started to head home.

## A WORLD OF POSSIBILITIES

Johnny found out that the ride-sharing company he was working for was having a get-together party for all of the drivers. Johnny was a little curious about meeting other drivers and wondered about what other types of men and women were also driving. He arrived at the hotel in LA and found the meeting room. They had lots of food and there were a few hundred drivers there. He looked around and saw people of just about every color and nationality you could imagine. Johnny got some water and a plate of fruit and next to him was a woman in her 30's.

Johnny asked her, "How long have you been driving?"

The woman introduced herself and said, "Hi, I'm Yolindy. I started driving 4 years ago but I wanted to travel, so I went to China and drove for the new company called Didi Chuxing."

"I heard Apple just invested a billion dollars in that company," Johnny replied.

He looked at Yolindy intently; she had short, jet-black hair, big puffy lips coated with fire engine red lipstick, and he suspected she was something of a wild-child when she was a little younger. She was dressed in black leather pants and a short sleeve blouse, which exposed tattoos on her arms that probably extended to her back. Completing the look were black combat boots.

Yolindy said, "Not only did I drive in China, but as I always wanted to go to Australia, so I drove there as well. I lived in Sidney for 4 months and drove a lot of men and women with cool accents."

Then Yolindy imitated an Australian accent by saying, "Okey-dokey mate," and they both laughed.

After Australia, she went to Europe and drove in Italy, France, Germany, and Switzerland. Yolindy said it was fun that she got to travel and she kept the cashflow coming in and made a lot of friends and got to see the world.

Johnny was fascinated about Yolindy's creativity to travel the world, so much so that he decided to hang out with her a little bit longer so he could learn more.

It was clear from the way she spoke that she was highly intelligent; she told Johnny that she had her MBA from Yale Business School, and for a while played around in the world of capital, climbing the corporate ladder. Finally she decided that she had had enough, and instead followed her dream of world travel. Yolindy obviously had many stories to tell from all of her different life experiences. Johnny asked her to talk about one of her more unusual driver rides.

"There was this drunken dickhead that I picked up from a bar in Australia," Yolindy explained. "As soon as he got into the car, he started hitting on me. He thought he was being so smooth by telling me how beautiful I was, and that I was so hot. I pulled up to his house and he started to try to massage my shoulders from the back seat. Bad move on his part."

It turned out that in addition to all of her other talents, Yolindy was also a black belt in Aikido, and so she was well prepared for any kind of situation that might arise.

"I grabbed one of the idiot's hands," Yolindy continued, "and just about broke it off."

"That put an end to any further 'massaging,' and the guy paid for his ride—no tip of course— got out of the car and basically slid away from the car, nursing his screwed-up hand!"

They both shared another good laugh.

Yolindy was a breath of fresh air with her attitude and living out her dreams. Johnny really enjoyed his conversation with her.

Johnny talked with a few other drivers and shared some stories with them. He looked at his phone because it was ringing, and he looked at the name—it was his agent. Johnny walked out of the meeting room into the hallway and answered.

His agent said in a very loud voice, "What the hell happened at the producer's pool?"

He started to reply, but before a word could come out of Johnny's mouth, the agent interrupted and said, "Johnny, you got the part."

Johnny couldn't believe it.

His agent again said, "Yes, you got the part. The producer liked you and said that you had your own opinions and that you were very authentic and not desperate like most of actors in Hollywood."

Johnny got a really good feeling through his whole body and a big smile came over his face. His agent told him to come to his office so he could sign the contract and hung up the phone.

Johnny stood there and he looked into the meeting rooms with all of the drivers and said a prayer for them all to have their dreams come true also.

Johnny thought that maybe he would drive in the near future, not because he needed the money, but because he enjoyed it so much. He would drive because it was kind of fun, and he would never forget what happened behind his closed car doors.

# RESOURCE PAGE

We think you may also enjoy the #1 best seller book called *Spiritual Cashflow* buy your copy on Amazon.com or order it at your local book store.

Do you want to write your own book? Or make your current book a *New York Times* best seller or Amazon best seller?

Give us an email at:
selawofpositivity@gmail.com
or call:
562-884-0062.

Check out these books: *How I Sold Millions of Books* and *Wake Up: Live the Life You Love.* Both books are available on Amazon.com so order your copy today.

www.ingramcontent.com/pod-product-compliance
Lightning Source LLC
Chambersburg PA
CBHW071006040426
42443CB00007B/687